WE THE PEOPLE

Spanish Colonies in America

by Alexandra Lilly

Content Adviser: Richard J. Bell, Ph.D.,
Assistant Professor, Department of History,
University of Maryland

Reading Adviser: Alexa L. Sandmann, Ed.D.,
Professor of Literacy, College and Graduate School of Education,
Kent State University

Compass Point Books ✦ Minneapolis, Minnesota

Compass Point Books
151 Good Counsel Drive
P.O. Box 669
Mankato, MN 56002-0669

This book was manufactured with paper containing at least 10 percent post-consumer waste.

On the cover: Hand-colored woodcut of Spanish mission in California

Photographs ©: North Wind Picture Archives, cover, 5, 6, 8, 17, 24, 26, 27, 29, 40; Prints Old and Rare, back cover (far left); Library of Congress, back cover, 20, 36, 37; The Granger Collection, New York, 7, 11, 12, 15, 19, 21, 28, 30, 35, 39, 41; MPI/Getty Images, 10; James Phelps/iStockphoto, 14; Nick Tzolov/iStockphoto, 22; Corbis, 34.

Editor: Jennifer VanVoorst
Page Production: Bobbie Nuytten
Photo Researcher: Svetlana Zhurkin
Cartographer: XNR Productions, Inc.
Library Consultant: Kathleen Baxter

Art Director: LuAnn Ascheman-Adams
Creative Director: Keith Griffin
Editorial Director: Nick Healy
Managing Editor: Catherine Neitge

Library of Congress Cataloging-in-Publication Data
Lilly, Alexandra.
  Spanish colonies in America / by Alexandra Lilly.
     p. cm. — (We the people)
  Includes index.
  ISBN 978-0-7565-3840-8 (library binding)
1. America—Discovery and exploration—Spanish—Juvenile literature. 2. Spain—Colonies—America—History—Juvenile literature. 3. Explorers—America—History—Juvenile literature. 4. Explorers—Spain—History—Juvenile literature. 5. Spaniards—America—History—Juvenile literature. I. Title. II. Series.
  E123.A44 2009
  970.01'6—dc22   2008011727

Visit Compass Point Books on the Internet at *www.compasspointbooks.com*
or e-mail your request to *custserv@compasspointbooks.com*

TABLE OF CONTENTS

SPANISH EXPLORATION

In 1492, King Ferdinand and Queen Isabella of Spain sponsored navigator Christopher Columbus in his historic voyage across the Atlantic Ocean. Columbus was searching for a sea route to Asia. Although he did not find such a passage, he did find lands that were unknown to Europeans at the time. These lands were rich in natural resources and opened up opportunities for Spain to conquer new territory and increase its wealth.

The Spanish were interested in gold and gems, as well as a quicker route to Asia and its spice market. They hoped that the lands Columbus found would eventually give them all three. By the early 1500s, Spain had set up bases on the islands of Cuba and Hispaniola as entry points to North America. Opportunities to explore the continent and gain its riches lay open to anyone who had the king's approval.

In 1513, King Ferdinand gave soldier and former colonial governor Juan Ponce de León the right to explore

4

Columbus' historic voyage led to Spain claiming most of the islands in the Caribbean.

the islands northwest of present-day Puerto Rico. Ponce de León was lured by legends of a magical "fountain of youth." He was also interested in the riches the new lands might hold. Sailing northwest, he landed at a point near present-day St. Augustine, Florida, and claimed the land for Spain.

5

Because it was Easter time, he named the land *Pascua Florida,* which meant "Feast of Flowers," the Spanish term for the Easter season. Ponce de León sailed along the coast of this land, which became known as La Florida. He charted the east coast of North America before returning to Puerto Rico in the fall.

Juan Ponce de León

In 1521, Ponce de León headed back to Florida, to the territory of the Calusa Indians. Ponce de León planned to set up a small colony on the Gulf of Mexico, and he brought with him 500 soldiers, priests, farmers, and craftsmen. Shortly after the colonists arrived, the Calusa attacked. After a bloody battle, Ponce de León and his colonists retreated to Cuba. He later died from a wound he received during the battle.

Ponce de León's settlement attempt was a failure, and the expeditions that followed were also unsuccessful. In 1527, conquistador Pánfilo de Narváez was chosen by Spain's King Charles V to establish a colony in Florida. Narváez landed near present-day Tampa Bay the following year with five ships and 400 soldiers. After landing, Narváez and most of his men continued on in search of

Narváez and his men landed in Tampa Bay on the Gulf of Mexico.

gold. They found some simple gold ornaments, but not enough to satisfy them. As the Spaniards traveled farther inland, they only found farming villages. The natives had no riches to speak of—no gold or silver or gems. The frustrated soldiers treated the natives cruelly. On one occasion, Narváez had the Calusa chief Ucita brought before him. When Ucita would not tell him where to find more gold, Narváez cut off his nose. This and similar acts made natives wary of Spanish troops.

Frustrated by his failure to find riches, Narváez decided to build large rafts and sail westward to Mexico, which was already under Spanish rule.

Spanish conquistadors searched the Florida wilderness for gold and other riches.

However, the rafts met with bad weather, and Narváez and most of his men drowned.

The survivors, Álvar Nuñez Cabeza de Vaca and three other members of the party, landed on the Gulf coast somewhere near Texas. It took eight years for them to reach Mexico City. This was the capital of New Spain, the Spanish empire in the New World. When they arrived in 1536, they told false tales of cities of gold and gems that they saw on their journey. Their stories convinced their fellow Spaniards that the legend of the Seven Cities of Gold was true. This legend originated in 1150 when the Moors conquered Mérida, Spain, and seven Catholic bishops fled the city. The bishops supposedly sailed west with caskets of gold and gems and founded seven cities of gold.

Fueled by the castaways' stories of treasure, Mexico City's Viceroy Antonio de Mendoza sent a Spanish priest north to look for the golden cities in 1539. The priest, Marcos de Niza, reported finding a trading center in present-day New Mexico called Cíbola. The city was rich

Cabeza de Vaca and his fellow survivors spent eight years traveling from the Gulf of Mexico to Mexico City.

with buffalo skins and turquoise, but there was no gold. However, Niza lied about the wealth the city held, claiming it was indeed one of the golden cities. In response, Mendoza chose conquistador Francisco Vásquez de Coronado to travel north in search of Cíbola to claim the city and its riches for Spain.

10

CLAIMING THE LAND

In 1540, Francisco Vásquez de Coronado and a group of 1,250 men headed north from Mexico City in search of the legendary golden cities. The 350 Spaniards and 900 natives traveled deep into the North American continent, beyond the lands previously visited by Europeans.

A 1534 painting of Spanish conquistadors in America with their horses and dogs

During the day, the Spaniards sweltered under the
hot desert sun, and they froze during the night. There was
little game to catch for food, and drinking water was scarce.
After more than four months of travel, Coronado's army
came upon the village of Cíbola that Niza had visited. But

*An 1848 illustration by Frederick Remington of Coronado and his soldiers
exploring the American Southwest*

the village was not as Niza had described, and Coronado was furious with the priest.

The meeting between the Spaniards and Cíbola's native Zuni Indians went badly. It turned into the first battle between a Native American tribe and a European army in the Southwest. Coronado's troops had horses, armor, and better weapons. The Zuni defended their lands with bows and arrows or stones. The Spaniards quickly defeated the natives and took over the town. Coronado told the Zuni that under Spanish rule they would have to become Christians. The Indians responded by packing their goods and fleeing the town.

Coronado continued searching the region, convinced that the land would yield riches. He and his men traveled through present-day Arizona, New Mexico, and parts of Texas, Colorado, Oklahoma, and Kansas. He claimed the land for Spain. Members of one of Coronado's scouting units became the first Europeans to see the Grand Canyon. Coronado's men also saw a muddy, reddish river that they named *Colorado*. They saw lands covered with bison, native villages, and fields of corn, beans, and squash. The Spaniards crossed cactus-filled deserts, sprawling grasslands, and several of America's great rivers—the Rio Grande, the Colorado, the Pecos, the Canadian, and the Arkansas. But

The Colorado River flows through the Grand Canyon; Colorado *means "red" in Spanish.*

they did not find gold.

While Coronado was traveling through the American Southwest, Juan Rodriguez Cabrillo was exploring the west coast. In 1542, Cabrillo became the first European to land in the present-day state of California. Cabrillo's crew of 250, traveling on the *San Salvador* and *Victoria*, sailed into the present-day San Diego harbor. The expedition continued northward and landed in the

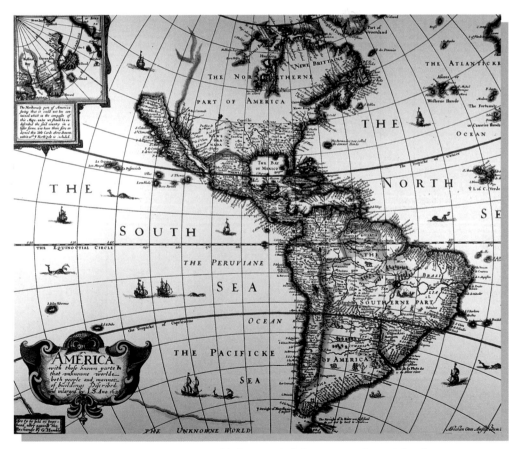

A 17th-century map of the New World depicts California as a large island.

Santa Barbara Channel, where they met members of the Chumash people. Cabrillo wrote in his journal, "We saw an Indian town on the land next to the sea, with large houses built much like those of New Spain. Many fine canoes, each with twelve or thirteen Indians came to the ships." Cabrillo's ships went as far north as the Russian River in northern California. The Cabrillo expedition pinpointed future sites for settlements in the land the Spanish called Alta California.

Meanwhile, Spaniards were again exploring the Southeast. King Charles of Spain had told conquistador Hernando de Soto to set up a Spanish colony in Florida. In 1539, de Soto foolishly landed near where Pánfilo de Narváez had landed years earlier. The natives had long memories and did not welcome de Soto's arrival.

To impress the natives, de Soto claimed to be an immortal sun god. Fearing the wrath of this armor-wearing god, the Timucua and the Apalachee Indians provided food for de Soto and his men and told them of rich tribes in the

De Soto and his soldiers set up camp upon arrival in Florida.

north. Over the next three years, de Soto ventured into the

Carolinas, and then went west to present-day Tennessee and

Alabama, claiming land for Spain as he went.

Like many conquistadors before him, de Soto was primarily interested in the wealth the new lands could bring him. As he traveled, de Soto tried to force natives to tell where they hid their riches. He captured the Choctaw chief Tuscaloosa and held him for ransom. But the Choctaws had a plan. Tuscaloosa told de Soto that the tribe's wealth was in the city of Mauvila. When de Soto and his men went to retrieve the treasure, they walked into an ambush. Although the Spaniards won the battle, they lost 20 men, as well as many possessions and horses.

De Soto and his men made a hasty retreat. Heading farther west, they came to the Mississippi River. After exploring the area of present-day Arkansas, de Soto died from a fever in the native village of Guachoya. The Spaniards could not risk the natives knowing about de Soto's death, since he was believed to be an immortal god. Rather than bury him, they added weights to his body and dumped him into the Mississippi River. Without their leader, de Soto's men decided it was time to go home.

De Soto and his men were ambushed by the Choctaws in the city of Mauvila—present-day Mobile, Alabama.

Although the expedition seemed to be a failure, it left a lasting mark on the land and the people. And de Soto had laid claim to a vast and varied land where Spain hoped to establish new colonies.

19

FOUNDING CITIES

Although Spain had claimed a great deal of land in the New World, it had settled very little of it. France and England seemed poised to colonize North America.

Spain's King Philip II realized Spain would need to establish a permanent presence in order to protect the land it had claimed.

In 1565, King Philip chose naval officer Pedro Menéndez de Avilés to establish a Spanish colony in Florida. On September 8, 1565, Menéndez de Avilés and a group of settlers landed on Florida's northeastern coast. They held

Pedro Menéndez de Avilés

20

a Mass of Thanksgiving for their safe arrival in the New World, followed by a feast and celebration with the local Timucua Indians. This celebration was the first recorded Thanksgiving ceremony in what would become the United States, more than 50 years before the Pilgrims' Thanksgiving at Plymouth. September 8, 1565, also marks the founding of the city of St. Augustine. The city is the oldest permanent European settlement in what is now the continental United States.

The first 100 St. Augustine settlers struggled to survive in the Florida wilderness. Mosquitoes buzzed in thick swarms. During

Pedro Menéndez de Avilés (center) led the building of St. Augustine in 1565.

21

the summer, the heat became oppressive. The settlers faced something they'd never experienced before—hurricanes. St. Augustine should have failed, but Menéndez de Avilés would not give up.

As city founder, Menéndez de Avilés served as governor, business manager, and military leader. He set up stone forts at St. Augustine and nearby San Mateo to protect those cities and the ships that traded there. Wooden

Fort Castillo de San Marcos in St. Augustine, Florida

22

forts and watchtowers dotted the coastline, keeping Florida towns safe from attack. Soon St. Augustine had become a trade center, selling Florida-produced vegetables, citrus fruits, and cattle.

With the city of St. Augustine, the Spanish finally had a permanent foothold in the Southeast. But the Southwest still remained unsettled. For decades, Spaniards had trekked through the region in search of gold and riches. In 1583, King Philip decided it was time to start a permanent colony in the region the Spaniards called New Mexico.

It took 15 years for an expedition to get under way. Explorer Juan de Oñate was chosen to lead the settlement effort. In January 1598, Oñate and about 600 settlers left for New Mexico. That summer, the settlers built their first town, San Gabriel, on the western bank of the Rio Grande River. Oñate served as governor of the New Mexico colony.

In 1608, one of Oñate's officers, Juan Martinez de Montoya, established a village called Santa Fe. When Pedro de Peralta became New Mexico's governor in 1610, he chose

The Governor's Palace in Santa Fe

Santa Fe to be the colonial capital. Santa Fe is the oldest capital city in the United States.

The Spaniards now had a base from which to explore the Southwest. They continued to look for gold, silver, and other natural treasures. Eventually, however, they saw that the value of New Mexico was not in gold or gems but in the land itself. New Mexico colonists traded leather, cattle, sheep, and salt. Eventually, New Mexico yielded silver and turquoise, but never enough to make Spaniards wealthy.

MISSION LIFE

During its time in North America, Spain did not flood its territories with Spanish settlers. Instead, it worked to make natives "Spanish." Spain wanted the native people to follow Spanish beliefs, honor the Spanish king, and pay Spanish taxes. The Spanish government sent priests and soldiers to America to achieve that goal.

Priests in Spain's colonies played many roles. They were religious leaders as well as explorers, builders, teachers, historians, and doctors. Their goal was to found missions, special communities that would convert the local people to Catholicism and teach them how to be good Spaniards. Natives were to learn the language, dress, religion, and work habits of Spaniards. They were to follow Spanish social structure. That meant that the Spaniards were rulers, landowners, and profit earners, while the natives provided labor.

The first missions were established in the 1690s by

Spanish soldiers, mission priests, and Native Americans prayed together.

Jesuit priests, under the leadership of Father Eusebio Kino.
These missions sprang up in present-day Arizona, New
Mexico, and Texas. Kino's plan called for central missions
in convenient locations, such as San Xavier del Bac near
Tucson. From there, priests visited local villages and
converted natives to Catholicism.

Another missionary movement took place in the 1700s in California. Spain had claimed territory in Alta California, but the land was not yet settled. Spain planned to settle this territory by setting up a string of missions. Father Junípero Serra was in charge of establishing these missions. Serra's first mission, San Diego de Alcalá, was founded in July 1769. Over the next 13 years, Serra

Spanish missions featured a chapel, as well as housing, kitchens, and work areas, which were grouped around a courtyard.

established eight more missions stretching north along a road that became known as El Camino Real, the "king's road." After Serra died in 1784, 12 more missions were founded. From San Diego de Alcalá in the south to San Francisco Solano de Sonoma in the north, the 21 missions spanned a distance of 700 miles (1,120 kilometers).

Father Junípero Serra traveled north along the "king's road," establishing missions as he went.

The Spanish priests who worked at the missions believed they were doing good things for the Indians, but many natives did not see it that way. Whether they wanted to or not, Native Americans were forced to give up their culture and their customs. They learned to farm the way Europeans did. They learned European trades such as blacksmithing or brickmaking. They were made to practice the Christian religion of the Spaniards.

Native Americans at the missions worked at crafts such as ropemaking and basket weaving.

Some Indians rebelled against the Spanish. Mission priests asked Spain to provide soldiers for protection. The soldiers lived in nearby forts called presidios. The presidios presented a problem for California's colonial government. Soldiers there needed a regular food supply. Governor Felipe de Neve came up with a plan: He would give away

Soldiers at the presidios often treated mission Indians harshly.

land to settlers who would grow food for the soldiers. The offer also included livestock, farming tools, and a clothing allowance. Additionally, settlers would not have to pay taxes for five years. In return, the new landowners were expected to sell their extra food crops to the presidios. Neve founded three towns under this plan: San José, Villa de Branciforte (today's Santa Cruz), and El Pueblo de Nuestra Señora la Reina de los Angeles de Porciúcula, known as Los Angeles.

Neve hoped to start Los Angeles with 24 married settlers and 34 married soldiers, plus families from Mexico. In 1781, only 12 families signed up to settle Los Angeles. Today the city is the second-largest in the United States.

The Spanish mission era lasted nearly 150 years. During this time, the native populations in Spanish-held territories dwindled. Native people suffered from living so closely with Europeans. They had no resistance to diseases such as measles, smallpox, whooping cough, and diphtheria. Disease and death became the common result of contact between Europeans and native people. In California, the

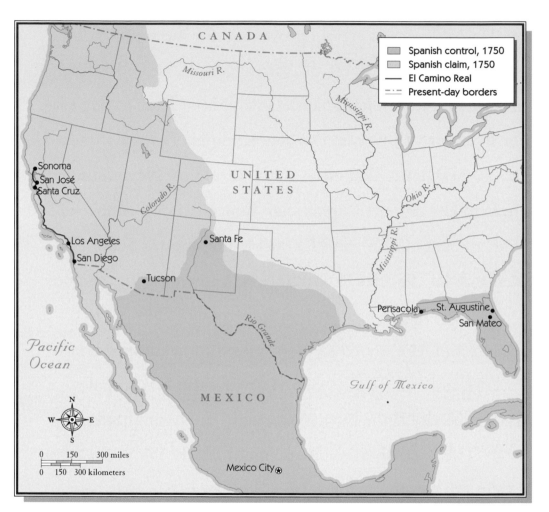

By the mid-1700s, Spain had claimed the majority of the American West.

native population fell by 75 percent—from 72,000 to 18,000. The death rate in Arizona, New Mexico, and Texas was even more dramatic.

INDEPENDENCE

Maintaining control of its colonies on the other side of the Atlantic Ocean was not an easy matter for Spain. From 1756 to 1763, the major powers in Europe were engaged in several wars, collectively named the Seven Years' War. During those years, Great Britain captured Cuba from Spain. In 1763, Spain gave Britain its territory in Florida in exchange for Cuba.

In 1776, the 13 British colonies located along America's Atlantic coast declared themselves independent from British rule. Those colonies formed the United States of America. Florida supported its British rulers. But when the Revolutionary War (1776–1783) ended, control of Florida returned to Spain. As the British left, Spanish colonists flooded into Florida.

During the War of 1812 (1812–1814), fought between the United States and Great Britain, Spain became an ally of the British. After the war, the United States sent

General Andrew Jackson into Florida to take over the city of Pensacola. Florida was becoming too much trouble for Spain. In 1821, Spain turned over all of Florida to the United States in the Adams-Onís Treaty. Florida became a state in 1845.

In 1810, the same spirit of liberty led Mexico's citizens to rebel against Spanish rule. The battle for Mexican independence lasted until 1821. At that point, California,

General Andrew Jackson and his troops took Pensacola from the Spanish in 1818.

Father Miguel Hidalgo led Mexico's 1810 revolt for independence from Spain.

Arizona, New Mexico, Texas, and parts of Nevada, Utah, and Colorado became part of Mexico.

In the early 1800s, the United States was involved in a period of westward expansion. Many Americans believed that it was America's destiny to control the land from the

Atlantic to the Pacific. Texas won its independence from Mexico in 1836 after the Battle of San Jacinto, and it existed as a separate nation for nine years. As part of his expansion program, President John Tyler signed an agreement to annex Texas in 1844. It became a state the following year.

In May 1846, the United States and Mexico went to war. The first battles took place in Texas, but the fighting

An 1836 illustration of Mexican leaders Antonio de Santa Anna and Perfecto de Cos surrendering to Texas leader Sam Houston

quickly spread along the Mexico-U.S. border region. Soon the entire Southwest was swept up in war. In 1848, the United States and Mexico signed the Treaty of Guadalupe Hidalgo, ending the Mexican War. With this treaty, Mexico gave up its territory in California, Texas, and parts of Arizona, New Mexico, Colorado, and Nevada. However, Mexicans living in those areas had the right to keep their land, customs, and language. Most chose to remain.

The Treaty of Guadalupe Hidalgo

California became a state in 1850. Nevada was admitted to the Union in 1864, and Colorado followed in 1876. Arizona and New Mexico did not become states until 1912.

A RICH HERITAGE

Spain left a rich heritage in its more than 300 years in America. The Spanish were the first to settle Florida, Texas, New Mexico, Arizona, and California. They gave us the names for California, Colorado, Florida, and Nevada— and dozens of towns in those states. The Spanish founded St. Augustine in 1565, the first European city in what became the United States. There Spaniards celebrated the first Thanksgiving. In New Mexico, they established the first capital city. These are the obvious legacies from the days when Spain ruled vast sections of today's America.

Lesser known is the relationship between Spanish rule and the Old West. It was the Spanish who brought horses to North America. Those horses became the basis for the herds of wild mustangs that once roamed the Great Plains. With horses, native tribes became more efficient bison hunters. They were also better able to defend their lands. Until the Spanish arrived, native tribes had hunted

Buffalo Hunt, *an 1825 lithograph after a painting by Peter Rindisbacher*

and fought on foot. They could not carry out major raids because they lacked the right kind of transportation. Horses turned Apaches and Comanches into cavalry units. On horseback and armed with European weapons, these tribes became the most feared warriors of the Southwest.

The Spanish also gave us cattle ranching. Before the Spanish colonized America, cattle ranching did not exist in the West. Many English words relating to cattle

39

Spanish settlers introduced cattle ranching to the West.

work come from the Spanish, including *ranch, lasso, corral, bronco*, and *chaps*.

But it was the promise of great riches that brought so many Spanish conquistadors to the New World. Although the Spanish never found the gold they sought, in the end it did exist. In the mid-1800s, gold rushes brought prospectors first to California and then to Colorado. Of course, Texas offered up "black gold"—oil. Mines in the Southwest have

Gold found in California proved that America did indeed hold the riches the Spanish conquistadors had been seeking.

also yielded copper, silver, turquoise, and other minerals.

Although only 14 percent of the U.S. population is Hispanic, one-third of Californians and Texans have Hispanic ancestry. Florida's Hispanic population tops 2 million people. Perhaps this is the true legacy of the Spanish colonies in America—its people.

GLOSSARY

ambush—surprise attack

cavalry—soldiers mounted on horseback

conquistador—Spanish conqueror

expedition—trip made for the purpose of exploration

Hispanic—coming from or relating to countries where Spanish is spoken

immortal—able to have eternal life or existence

Jesuit—member of a religious group of priests founded by St. Ignatius of Loyola

legacies—things that are handed down from one generation to another

prospectors—people who search for gold

viceroy—governor who represents a king in a province or colony

DID YOU KNOW?

- El Camino Real, the road traveled by Father Junípero Serra, still exists today and is the main street in many California cities.

- The routes traveled by pioneers moving West were the same routes traveled by Hernando de Soto in 1539–1542. Those routes had been used for centuries by natives.

- In addition to soldiers and horses, the de Soto expedition also included seeds, nails, axes, saws, bloodhounds, and a herd of pigs.

- During his time in California, Father Junípero Serra visited every Spanish mission in the colony. Serra traveled a total of 24,000 miles (38,400 km) over 14 years.

- St. Augustine's oldest house still standing was built in about 1706 and is currently a museum.

- The history of oranges in Florida can be traced back to St. Augustine in 1579. Nearly 200 years later, Franciscan monks introduced oranges to the mission gardens in California. Those early citrus fruits were sour oranges, not the flavorful, sweet juice oranges of today.

IMPORTANT DATES

Timeline

1492	Columbus lands on Hispaniola in the Caribbean Sea and claims the land for Spain.
1513	Ponce de León lands in present-day Florida.
1527	Narváez's expedition fails in Florida.
1539	De Soto begins his exploration of the Southeast.
1540	Coronado begins his exploration of the Southwest.
1542	Cabrillo explores Alta California.
1565	St. Augustine becomes the first permanent European settlement in North America.
1769	Father Serra founds the first California mission at San Diego de Alcalá.
1821	Mexico wins independence from Spain.
1848	Mexico cedes California, Arizona, New Mexico, Nevada, and Colorado to the United States in the Treaty of Guadalupe Hidalgo.

IMPORTANT PEOPLE

HERNANDO DE SOTO (1496?—1542)

Spanish conquistador who explored Nicaragua and parts of South America; in 1537, he became governor of Cuba with the right to conquer Florida; in search of gold and great riches, he explored from present-day Tampa, Florida, throughout the Southeast to the Mississippi River

FATHER JUNÍPERO SERRA (1713–1784)

Spanish priest who personally founded nine missions in California; in 1769, Serra set off on an expedition, called the Sacred Expedition, to establish a series of missions along the California coast; Serra was in charge of all the missions that ran along El Camino Real, from San Diego to Sonoma

EUSEBIO KINO (1645–1711)

Italian priest charged with founding missions in the New World; Kino was also an astronomer, a mathematician, and a mapmaker; he is credited with drawing the first accurate maps of northwestern Mexico, California's Baja Peninsula, and lower Arizona

FRANCISCO VÁSQUEZ DE CORONADO (1510–1554)

Spanish nobleman who explored the Southwest in search of the golden city of Cíbola; he became a viceroy of a region in New Spain but lost that position after a rebellion by local native people; he was later a member of Mexico City's government

WANT TO KNOW MORE?

More Books to Read

Burgan, Michael. *The Spanish Conquest of America.* New York: Chelsea
House Publications, 2007.

Doak, Robin S. *Coronado: Francisco Vásquez de Coronado Explores the
Southwest.* Minneapolis: Compass Point Books, 2002.

Mountjoy, Shane. *St. Augustine.* New York: Chelsea House Publications, 2007.

Wilson, Lenore. *The Spanish Exploration of the Southwest.* Philadelphia:
Mason Crest Publishers, 2003.

On the Web

For more information on this topic, use FactHound.

1. Go to *www.facthound.com*

2. Type in this book ID: 0756538408

3. Click on the *Fetch It* button.

FactHound will find the best Web sites for you.

On the Road

Mission San Luis Rey

4050 Mission Ave.

Oceanside, CA 92057

760/757-3651

The largest of the California
missions includes a museum,
cemetery, and gardens

Fort Matanzas

8635 A1A S.

St. Augustine, FL 32080

904/471-0116

Historic fort with exhibits, guided
tours, and nature trails

Look for more We the People books about this era:

African-Americans in the Colonies

The California Missions

Dutch Colonies in America

English Colonies in America

The French and Indian War

French Colonies in America

The Jamestown Colony

The Mayflower Compact

The Plymouth Colony

The Salem Witch Trials

The Stamp Act of 1765

The Thirteen Colonies

Williamsburg

Women of Colonial America

A complete list of We the People titles is available on our Web site:
www.compasspointbooks.com

INDEX

About the Author

Alexandra Lilly writes children's nonfiction books. She enjoys digging into history
and discovering new and interesting aspects of our American heritage. Lilly is
also interested in the culture and people of foreign countries. She lived in Canada
and Australia before settling in the foothills of the Blue Ridge Mountains. Lilly is
married and has four sons and a charming dog named Sydney.